A New True Book

BEAVERS

By Emilie U. Lepthien

CHILDRENS PRESS®
CHICAGO

North American beaver

Project Editor: Fran Dyra
Design: Margrit Fiddle

PHOTO CREDITS
H. Armstrong Roberts—© D. Gleiter, 22
© Jerry Hennen—15 (right), 43 (top)
© Emilie Lepthien—21
North Wind Picture Archives—38 (top)
Photri—25
© James P. Rowan—38 (bottom)
Tom Stack & Associates—© Nancy Adams, 32
TSW-CLICK/Chicago—© Millard Sharp, 4 (top
left); © Leonard Lee Rue III, 33; © David
Woodward, 44
Valan—© J. A. Wilkinson, Cover, 10, 17, 18
(right); © Wayne Lankinen, 2, 4 (bottom left), 9
(bottom), 18 (left), 39, 37 (left), 40, 43 (bottom
left); © John Fowler, 4 (bottom right); © Robert
C. Simpson, 4 (top right); © Dennis W. Schmidt,
6 (left), 9 (top), 24; © Stephen J. Krasemann, 12
(right), 19, 26 (right); © Esther Schmidt, 16;
© Michael J. Johnson, 20; © Wils Schurig, 37
(left); © Val & Alan Wilkinson, 45
Visuals Unlimited—© John D. Cunningham, 5,
28, 43 (center); © Irene Vandermolen, 6 (right),
15 (left); © Science Visuals Unlimited, 12 (left);
© W.A. Banaszewski, 13, 14 (right), 41; © Tim
Cunningham, 14 (left); © Carlyn Galati, 26 (left);
© Leonard Lee Rue III, 35; © Tom J. Ulrich, 43
(bottom center); © Len Rue, Jr., 43 (bottom
right)
Diagram by Tom Dunnington—28
Cover—Beaver

Library of Congress Cataloging-in-Publication Data

Lepthien, Emilie U. (Emilie Utteg)
  Beavers / by Emilie U. Lepthien.
    p.   cm. — (A New true book)
  Includes index.
  Summary: An introduction to the physical
characteristics, habits, and natural environment of the
beaver.
  ISBN 0-516-01131-6
    1. Beavers—Juvenile literature. [1. Beavers.]
I. Title.
QL737.R632L46   1992
599.32'32—dc20   92-14909
                                      CIP
                                      AC

TABLE OF CONTENTS

Mice, rats, squirrels, and muskrats (clockwise from top left)
are some of the many kinds of rodents. More than half
of the world's mammals are rodents.

WHAT IS A BEAVER?

Beaver cutting
down a tree

Beavers are the largest
rodents, or gnawing
mammals, in North America.
Rodents include mice, rats,
squirrels, and muskrats,
as well as beavers.

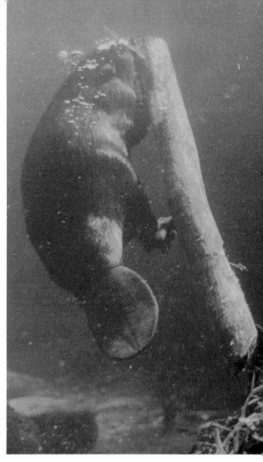

Beavers cut up fallen trees
to make shorter logs. Then
they carry the logs underwater
to their dam.

Beavers live near
wooded areas in lakes,
rivers, and streams. More
beavers live in North
America than anywhere
else in the world.

The North American beaver's scientific name is *castor canadensis*. The name "castor" comes from "castoreum," a yellow substance made by glands near the beaver's tail. Castoreum has a strong scent. It is often used to make perfume.

WHAT DO BEAVERS EAT?

Beavers eat the bark, twigs, and leaves of trees. They prefer willow, birch, aspen, and poplar trees.

In spring and summer, beavers eat marsh grasses, the roots of water plants, clover, and berries.

Trees provide food for beavers. They like to eat bark (above) and leaves (below).

THE BODY OF A BEAVER

Beavers have a thick, furry body and a flat, wide tail that looks like a paddle. A beaver may grow to be 3 to 4 feet long and weigh between 40 and 95 pounds. Beavers continue to grow as long as they live.

Beavers have small eyes and ears and strong jaws.

A beaver carrying a cut branch (left) in its teeth. Because the front of the incisors (right) do not wear down as quickly as the back, the incisors are shaped like chisels

They have twenty teeth— ten in each jaw. The four front teeth are used for gnawing. They are called incisors. Beavers use these sharp teeth to cut down trees. These front teeth continue to grow throughout a beaver's life.

Beavers have sixteen back teeth called molars. These teeth are used for chewing and grinding. There is a large space between the incisors and the molars.

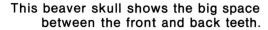
This beaver skull shows the big space between the front and back teeth.

13

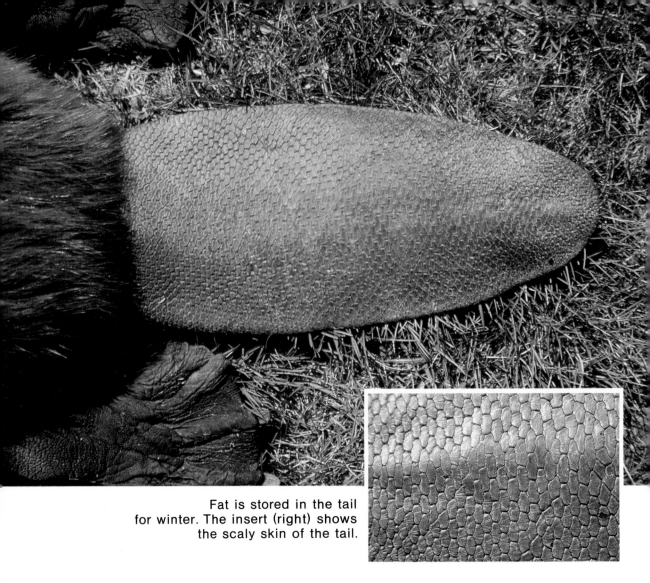

Fat is stored in the tail
for winter. The insert (right) shows
the scaly skin of the tail.

Their flat tail is covered
with black, scaly skin. It is
12 to 18 inches long and
about 6 inches wide.

A swimming beaver steers with its tail. A beaver slaps the surface of the water with its tail (inset) to warn other beavers of danger.

When beavers swim,
they use their tail to steer.
They slap their tail on the
water to warn other beavers
of danger.

A beaver stands on its hind legs while cutting down trees.

The tail is used on land, too. When beavers stand on their hind legs to cut down trees, their tail supports them like another leg.

Beaver fur is yellowish

brown or dark brown. Long guard hairs form the outer coat. The guard hairs protect the soft, thick underfur. The underfur traps air next to the beaver's skin and helps

Some very old, fat beavers may weigh as much as 100 pounds.

The beaver's front feet (right) are almost like hands. They can carry sticks, stones, and other objects. Beavers take very good care of their fur coats. They comb the fur with their hind feet (above).

the animal stay warm in the water. Beavers comb their fur with two split nails on each hind foot.

Beavers' front legs are short, and the front feet are small. Their hind legs are long and strong.

Their webbed hind feet help make beavers good swimmers.

WHAT MAKES BEAVERS SPECIAL?

Beavers have special body parts, or adaptations, that help them swim and work underwater. Their hind feet have five long, webbed toes. The webbed feet are good for swimming.

Beavers cannot see well at a distance.
They depend on their good hearing and
sense of smell to warn of danger.

Their nostrils and ears can
be closed off by special
muscles, so beavers can
stay underwater for as long
as fifteen minutes.

They also have a
transparent inner eyelid
that covers and protects

Beavers are strong, graceful, swift swimmers.

their eyes so they can see underwater.

And a beaver has two flaps of skin behind its protruding front teeth. These flaps draw together to seal off the back of its mouth while it gnaws wood or works in the water.

A beaver dam in Colorado. Some beaver dams
are more than 1,000 feet (305 meters) long.

NATURE'S BUILDERS

Beavers are always working. They build their dams across narrow streams. They use their short front feet to push mud and stones into a ridge. Then they push sticks and logs into the muddy ridge to build up the dam.

Beavers cut down small trees—such as pines or

This tree is almost ready to fall.

birches–with their front teeth.
To bring down a tree,
a beaver makes a deep
cut all around the tree
with its strong front teeth.
Then it makes a second
cut about three inches

below the first. The beaver chews away at the wood between these two cuts until it has cut through the trunk. When the tree is down, the beaver gnaws off all the branches.

When you see tree stumps with pointed tops, you know that beavers have been at work.

A beaver in a canal (left). Another beaver (above) tows a branch to its dam.

When trees are near the stream, the beavers drag or roll them into the water. When trees are farther away, the beavers dig water channels called canals. Then they float the trees down to the stream.

Beavers usually work on their dams at night. They build their dams high enough and wide enough to keep water from flowing over or around them.

Soon a pond forms behind the dam. The pond may be 3 to 6 feet deep. Then the beaver family can build a lodge with an underwater entrance in the middle of the pond.

From the outside, a beaver lodge looks like a pile of brush in the water.
But inside, the beavers are warm and dry in a cozy den.

Pond surface

Tunnel entrance

THE LODGE

A beaver lodge is a mound of logs, branches, and mud. Its top rises above the water level. The entrance is an underwater tunnel, which keeps enemies out.

The roof is loosely covered with branches so air can get into the lodge. Before winter comes, the beavers add more layers to the roof and smear it

Inside their lodge, beavers make beds of wood chips and grasses.

with mud. This keeps the lodge warm and dry, even during the heaviest snows and coldest weather.

Inside the lodge, the beavers build ledges above the water level. The ledges are covered with a thick layer of wood chips and grasses. The beavers sleep on these dry ledges. The whole beaver family helps keep the dam and lodge in good repair.

If a river or lake is too deep, the beavers cannot build a dam. Then they burrow, or dig, into the riverbank and build a roomy den. The entrance is underwater, and the tunnel leads upward to the den in the riverbank, high above the water level.

Male and female beavers stay together for life.

FAMILY LIFE

Beavers mate for life. They usually mate in January or February. About three months later, two to four babies, called kits,

are born. The kits weigh
about one pound at birth.
They are covered with fur
and their eyes are open.
They have small teeth, and
they can swim almost
immediately.

Adult beaver with a seven-day-old kit

Like all mammals, the kits drink their mother's milk. When they are only a few days old, kits are able to eat plants. Kits usually stay with their parents until they are two years old.

By autumn, the youngest kits are ready to work with their parents and older brothers and sisters.

Beavers do not hibernate, or sleep through the winter, so they must gather a food supply. They store twigs and branches underwater near the lodge entrance. The cold water

A beaver visits its underwater food supply near its lodge.

keeps the leaves and branches fresh.

To protect their dams and lodges from other beavers, the whole family builds piles of plants and mud on the shore. They mark these piles with scent to establish their boundaries.

In spring, the parents urge the older offspring to find their own homes. Some two-year-old beavers

The entire beaver family
works to keep their
dam in good repair.

travel long distances to
find a new building site or
an abandoned lodge and
dam in need of repair.
Many are killed by
predators on the way. But
beavers often live to be
twelve years old.

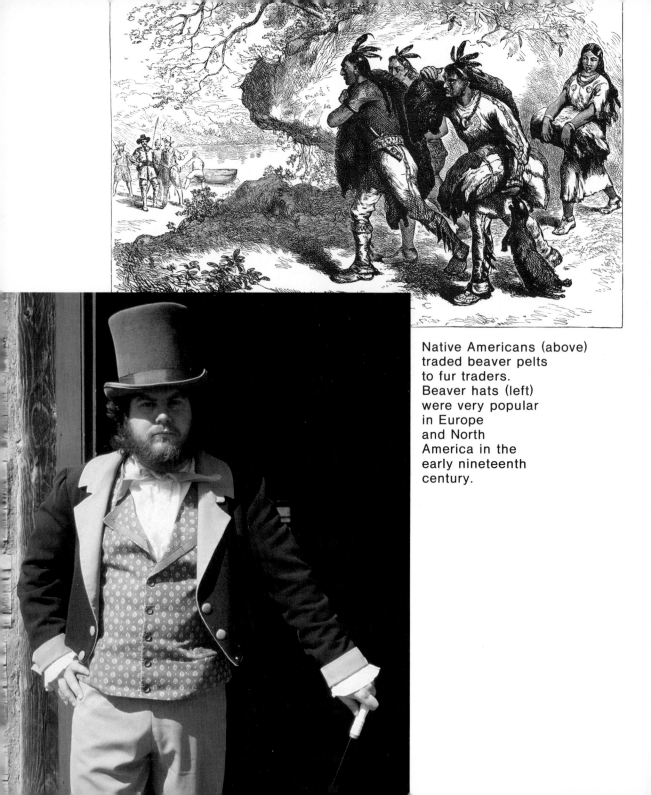

Native Americans (above)
traded beaver pelts
to fur traders.
Beaver hats (left)
were very popular
in Europe
and North
America in the
early nineteenth
century.

FURS AND FORTUNES

Beavers played an important part in North American history. In the 1700s and 1800s, hats made of beaver fur became popular, and high prices were paid for beaver pelts. Trappers hunted beaver throughout the western United States and much of Canada. By the late 1800s, these

beautiful animals were
almost extinct, or wiped out.
   In many states, beavers
are now protected by law.
They have been reintroduced
in northeastern states to
assist in water conservation.

Permits are needed to trap beavers today, and they can be trapped only at certain times of the year. Dams and lodges cannot be removed without a permit.

Sometimes beavers flood roads with their ponds or cut down trees that are valuable to people. Then they can be caught in safe traps like this one and released in places where they can live without causing damage.

HOW BEAVERS HELP US

Beavers are valuable in many ways. For example, silt builds up in the ponds behind their dams. When the beavers move on, the dam breaks down. As the water drains, the silt enriches the soil, and a fertile valley is left.

Beaver ponds create needed wetlands. These wetlands become habitats for waterfowl, mink, muskrats, and otters.

Beaver ponds provide homes for many different kinds of
animals, such as Canada geese (top) and (bottom, left to
right) ducks, mink, and otters.

Beaver lodge and pond. Beavers live in the water to defend themselves from enemies and to be near their food supply.

People today know that beavers are important to our environment. Although these amazing animals may sometimes damage forests and farmland, they also do much to improve our world.

WORDS YOU SHOULD KNOW

abandoned (uh•BAN•dund)—left behind; deserted

adaptations (ah•dap•TAY•shunz)—special body parts that enable an animal to do certain things or to live in certain places

boundaries (BOUN•dreez)—edges; the lines that mark off an area

burrow (BER•oh)—to dig in the ground

canal (kuh•NAL)—a channel or ditch dug into the ground and filled with water

castor canadensis (KASS•ter can•uh•DEN•sis)—the scientific name for the North American beaver

castoreum (kass•TOR•ee•um)—a yellow substance produced by beavers

conservation (kahn•ser•VAY•shun)—saving; the preservation of natural things such as water or trees

dam (DAM)—a structure built across a stream to control the flow of water

extinct (ex•TINKT)—no longer living

fertile (FER•til)—rich; able to produce abundant crops

gland (GLAND)—a special body part that makes things that the body can use or give off

gnaw (NAW)—to bite and wear away with the teeth

habitat (HAB•ih•tat)—the place where an animal is usually found

hibernate (HY•ber•nayt)—to go into a state of deep sleep in which body temperature drops and breathing slows

incisors (in•SY•zerz)—long, sharp, front teeth

kits (KITS)—beaver babies

ledge (lehj)—a flat structure that comes out from a wall like a shelf

mammal (MAM•il)—one of a group of warm-blooded animals that have hair and nurse their young with milk

molars (MO • lerz) — broad, flat back teeth

offspring (AWF • spring) — young; children

pelt (PELT) — the fur and skin of a mammal

permit (PER • mit) — a paper that says a person is allowed to do a certain thing

pond (PAHND) — a small, shallow lake

predator (PREH • dih • ter) — an animal that kills and eats other animals

protruding (pro • TROO • ding) — sticking out

reintroduce (re • in • troh • DOOS) — to bring back again

rodent (ROH • dint) — an animal that has long, sharp front teeth for gnawing

silt (SILT) — small bits of sand, rock, and mud carried along by water

site (SITE) — a place or location, especially a place where something is built

transparent (tranz • PAIR • uhnt) — so clear that it can be seen through

tunnel (TUH • nil) — a hole that makes a path through the ground

webbed (WEBBD) — joined by broad flaps of skin

wetland (WET • land) — an area of land that is covered with shallow water

INDEX

About the Author

Emilie U. Lepthien received her BA and MS degrees and certificate in school administration from Northwestern University. She taught upper-grade science and social studies, wrote and narrated science programs for the Chicago Public Schools' station WBEZ, and was principal in Chicago, Illinois, for twenty years. She received the American Educator's Medal from Freedoms Foundation.

She is a member of Delta Kappa Gamma Society International, Chicago Principals' Association, Illinois Women's Press Association, National Federation of Press Women, and AAUW.

She has written books in the Enchantment of the World, New True Books, and America the Beautiful series.